CHRISTMAS
Program Builder

No. 45

Graded resources for the
creative program planner

Compiled by Paul M. Miller

For the most practical use of this material, it is suggested the group using the booklet obtain at least
three copies: one to be used by the director, and the
others to be clipped for participants. This material
is protected by copyright laws.

LILLENAS PUBLISHING COMPANY
Kansas City, MO 64141

Christmas Gifts

ALL: We feel rich in gifts—

CHILD 1: Happiness too,

CHILD 2: Knowing this Christmas

CHILD 3: We have YOU!

CHILD 4: Enjoy this season,

CHILD 5: Be glad it's come,

CHILD 6: Celebrate God's gift,

ALL: His only Son . . . Jesus!

—Evangeline Carey

The Animals

CHILD 1:
  The donkey in the stable,
  He saw Jesus born.

CHILD 2:
  The sheep were in the meadow
  And heard the angels' song.

CHILD 3:
  The cow lent Him her manger
  That first Christmas morn.

CHILD 4:
  The camels saw Him later;
  They brought three kings along.

CHILD 5:
  Moo, neigh, baa.
  Merry Christmas everyone.

—Judith McFerren

King of Glory

Christ is born
  Our King of Glory,
Now you know
  The Christmas story.

—Robert Colbert

Real Glad

Just a manger
For a bed
  Is all the Savior had,
But just to know
That He was born,
  Makes my heart real glad.

—Robert Colbert

Go Tell It

Go tell it on the mountain!
  Tell it on the sea!
Jesus was born on Christmas Day.
Born to save you! *(Gestures toward congregation)*
Born to save me! *(Points to self)*

—Helen Kitchell Evans

My Plan

(Child carries a large heart out and then lays it on the altar before leaving.)

I give my heart to Jesus.
  I just want to say,
I plan to follow Jesus
  As I grow each day.

—Helen Kitchell Evans

That First Christmas

A sky full of angels
And a big, bright star
Brought men to see Jesus
From near and from far.

—*Margaret Primrose*

Merry Christmas to You!

May your Christmas
Have just the right touch,
Of joy and happiness,
Because God loves you so much!

—*Evangeline Carey*

Christmas Welcome

We welcome everyone here.
We're glad you've come this year.
Merry Christmas to you
(Gestures toward audience)
And you and you and you.

—*Judith McFerren*

Animals from That First Christmas Night

(Recitation for six children. Costuming is easy if you use large sheets of poster board in appropriate colors. Draw the faces of the animals on the poster board, then cut out a hole the size of a child's face in each poster board. The children hold them in front of their face and look through them.)

CHILD 1:

I am the lamb
That was asleep on the hay,
When a light shone so brightly,
It turned night into day.

CHILD 2:

I am the cow
That was asleep for the night,
When Mary and Joseph
Came into my sight.

CHILD 3:

I am the donkey
Who shared the stall.
I had to move over
And make room for them all.

CHILD 4:

I am the camel
Who watched the sky.
I carried the wise men
To where Baby Jesus lie.

CHILD 5:

I am a lamb
Who lay in the straw.
I saw the wise men worship Jesus;
On their knees they did fall.

CHILD 6:

I am the shepherd's dog
Who was out on the hill.
I heard the angels sing.
Oh my, what a thrill!

ALL:

We are the animals
From that long ago night.
We came to share Jesus
And tell of that sight!
Jesus was born in Bethlehem
On that first Christmas night!

—*Janet S. Teitsort*

God Bless Your Christmas

May your holiday season
Be endlessly blessed,
Filled with lots of love,
The very, very best!

—*Evangeline Carey*

Jesus' First Bed

Because Mary and Joseph
Needed somewhere to stay,
Baby Jesus was born
On a bed of hay.

—*Margaret Primrose*

Lamb of Gold

CHILD 1:
Welcome, welcome, Christmas morn
Christ our Lord and King is born.

CHILD 2:
He who takes our sins away
Lies in a manger filled with hay.

CHILD 3:
Welcome, welcome, holy birth
Heaven's joy now visits Earth.

CHILD 4:
God the Father gives His Son
Long-awaited, promised One.

CHILD 5:
Sing with a glad, joyous refrain
Worship now His holy name.

CHILD 6:
Love, peace, new hope He brings.
Loudly let creation sing.

CHILD 7:
Honor now our Lamb of Gold
Firstling of the heavenly fold.

CHILD 8:
God and man unite in Christ
To bless us with eternal life.

—*Robert Colbert*

Ashley

Jesus Christ Is Born Today!

May you share the beauty of this
season,
Because Jesus is born today.
He came to be our Savior
And take our sins away.

Praise Him with all your heart,
Give Him honor too,
Because Jesus Christ has come,
And He loves YOU!

—*Evangeline Carey*

★ C-H-R-I-S-T-M-A-S

*(Children carry letters. An option
would be to have the children carry letters made from bread stick dough.)*

CHILD 1: **C** is for the Christ child

CHILD 2: **H** e comes to us today,

CHILD 3: **R** eady now to enter,

CHILD 4: **I** n our hearts to stay.

CHILD 5: **S** ongs we sing to Jesus,

CHILD 6: **T** elling of our love.

CHILD 7: **M** ay we ever serve Him

CHILD 8: **A** nd praise God above.

CHILD 9: **S** avior, we will follow
Your path every day.

ALL: Give us help and guidance
All along the way.

—*Helen Kitchell Evans*

Welcome

Welcome to our program;
I see you're happy too.
Thank you much for smiling;
I have a big job to do.

You can help me with my part.
Just keep wishing with all your heart
That I won't forget to say:
You're welcome here this Christmas
Day.
(Pause)
Thank you.

—*Theodoris G. Smith*

Christmas Bells

(Sung to the tune of "Jingle Bells")

VERSE:

In a manger long ago,
On Christmas Eve you see,
Jesus Christ was born,
From sin to set us free.
There were wise men three,
Down on bended knee,
And then the shepherds did proclaim
The greatest news on earth!

CHORUS:

Oh! Christmas bells, Christmas bells,
Ring them loud and clear.
Tell the story of Jesus' love
For everyone to hear.

(Repeat chorus)

—*Wanda E. Brunstetter*

— Casey

Many Years Ago

Surely Christ was born
  Many years ago,
Because the Bible
  Tells us so.
The holy angel
  Proclaimed His birth,
Goodwill to men,
  And peace on earth.

—*Robert Colbert*

Why I Like Christmas

CHILD 1: *(Wearing a big nose)*

I like the *smells* of Christmas;
  The spicy smell of cookies,
  The waxy smell of candles,
  The piney smell of Christmas
  trees.

CHILD 2: *(Wearing big ears)*

I like the *sounds* of Christmas:
  The tinkling sound of bells,
  The whispering sounds of se-
  crets,
  The happy sounds of carols.

CHILD 3: *(Wearing big gloves)*

I like the *feel* of Christmas:
  The softness of the snow,
  The coldness of the wind,
  The warmth of the fire.

CHILD 4: *(Wearing big glasses)*

I like the looks of Christmas;
  The sparkle of the tinsel,
  The wrappings on the presents,
  The winking of the lights.

ALL:

But, best of all, we like
  The joy of knowing Jesus,
  The peace of His forgiveness,
  And the love of God, who sent
  Him.

—*Marita M. Moore*

Never Change

The story is old;
  It will never change.
Oh, thank God,
  It remains the same.

A Babe is born in Bethlehem
  In a manger, a stable so low,
But He is the Savior of the world,
  Yes, I know it is so.

A Baby is born in Bethlehem
  The story remains the same
How Jesus came to save our souls.
  Thank God, it will never change.

—*Theodoris G. Smith*

Looking for Christmas

CHILD 1:

(Holding a cookie jar) _Cody_

I looked in the cookie jar,
  Filled to the brim,
But I didn't find Christmas,
  Just cookies with trim.

CHILD 2:

(Holding a Christmas stocking) _Josh_

I looked in my stocking,
  Hanging in its place.
I found an orange and apple,
  But Christmas? Not a trace!

CHILD 3:

(Holding a Christmas package) _Casey_

I looked in a package,
  Underneath the tree.
But I didn't find Christmas;
  It was only socks for me.

CHILD 4:

(Holding a manger scene) _Gabriella_

Then I saw the manger,
  Dollhouse size, so small.
I found the meaning of Christmas;
  Baby Jesus was in the stall!

—*Janet S. Teitsort*

May God Bless You This Christmas!

Cody

May your Christmas
Be full of joy,
Filled to the brim,
Make Jesus your celebration,
And be blessed by HIM!

—Evangeline Carey

Worship Him

Erica

The shepherd and wise men
Knew just what to do
When they heard of the birth
Of the King of the Jews.
They brought gifts of worship
And they spread the good news.
So this Christmas season
Won't you worship Him too?

—Brenda Wood

Christmas

Why are sleigh bells ringing,
Carolers singing,
People bringing gifts to those they
    love?
  It's Christmas!

Why are bells in heaven ringing,
Hosts in glory singing,
Angels bringing the news of God's
    gift of love?
  It's Christmas!

Why are church bells pealing,
The saints kneeling?
People bringing their praise to the
    infant King?
  It's Christmas!

Why are bells in my heart ringing,
My spirit singing?
My life I am bringing to Jesus, my
    Savior King.
  It's Christmas!

—Elizabeth Craig Haynes

Clip Clop

(Slap thighs for sound effect.)

ALL:
Clip, clop, clip, clop
  All the day.
Clip, clop, clip, clop
  All the way.

FIRST WISE MAN:
We know that riding camels
  Is not a lot of fun,
But God has led us by a star
  To see His newborn Son.

SECOND WISE MAN:
We've offered gold and perfume.
  To Mary's baby boy.
We've bent our knees and worshiped.
  It's really been a joy.

THIRD WISE MAN:
God warned us in a dream tonight
  That trouble has begun.
King Herod wants to harm the
    Child,
  And we had better run.

ALL:
Clip, clop, clip, clop
  Through the night.
Clip, clop, clip, clop
  Out of sight.

—Margaret Primrose

7

The Shepherd Boy

(CHILD 1 *wears short brown shepherd's robe and sandals.* CHILD 2 *could carry a cardboard lamb or be dressed as a sheep.*)

CHILD 1:

I am a simple shepherd-child;
My job is tending sheep.
I keep a close, close watch on them
Wherever they may leap.
If a sheep should go astray,
I'll look before I sleep.

CHILD 2:

Jesus says I am His sheep,
His job to care for me.
My soul He also wants to keep
If I will love Him too.
I know someday I will leap
To meet Him up in heaven.

—*Judith McFerren*

Sights of Christmas

Josh

At Christmas we see cards and gifts
And wreaths and lights and tree;
But let's not lose sight of Jesus
Who was sent for you and me.

—*Brenda Wood*

Grandpa's Gift

My grandpa's very special
So I want my gift to be
Something very very special
Just to him and just from me.

I wrapped my newest color book
To put beside the tree.
He'll be so glad to see it,
I can hardly wait to see.

(May substitute "grandma," "fire truck," etc., if needed)

—*Margaret Primrose*

The Gift with Meaning

(Choral for two groups)

GROUP 1: Stockings and tinsel

GROUP 2: Trees lit up with light,

GROUP 1: Symbols of Christmas

GROUP 2: A wonderful sight.

GROUP 1: Then there's the manger in stable dim
Shepherds, a star, God's Holy Son.

GROUP 2: A baby, a Savior come to offer us peace,
Forgiveness, joy, and a new life begun.

GROUP 2: So, light up the tree lights
Gift giving is fun.

GROUP 1: Tradition *(short pause)* with meaning

ALL: In the gift of God's Son.

—*C. R. Scheidies*

⭐ The Best Christmas Present

CHILD 1: Lots of presents 'neath the tree,
A bunch of them are meant for me.
I want them all, but they're not the reason
We celebrate this Christmas season.

CHILD 2: I like to give to those I love
A toy, a book, a shirt, or glove.
I like to see smiles, but they're not the reason
We celebrate this Christmas season.

CHILD 3: The best present is one of love.
God sent His Son down from above;
He's the reason
For the season.

—Judith McFerren

Shaylyne

Just to Say "Hi!"

I have been chosen to say "Hi!"
We're mighty glad to see you.
We've planned a little program;
We hope that it will please you.

(If given by a boy, have him wave to congregation. If a girl, have her curtsey—old-fashioned but wins smiles.)

—Helen Kitchell Evans

Joyful Words

CHILD 1:

"Peace on earth," the angel said,
And when the shepherds heard,
They ran to find the Prince of Peace,
And spread the joyful word.

CHILD 2:

They called their friends to come and
see
The Baby in the hay,
Sent by God as future King;
Born on Christmas Day.

—Millie Barger

Gabriella

The Little Town

The little town
Of Bethlehem
Was blessed
With heavenly light,
For all about
The stable shone
The Father's glory bright.
An Infant wrapped
In swaddling clothes
Who in a manger lay,
Was worshiped by those
Who did behold
That first Christmas Day.

—Robert Colbert

A Special Star

I love to look at Christmas trees,
  With twinkly lights so bright.
They make me think of a special
    star,
  That shone upon that night.

—Janet S. Teitsort

Our Jesus

*(For three boys, the first one small, the
second middle-sized, and the third the
tallest, and one girl.)*

BOY 1: *(Carrying a doll wrapped
    in a blanket)*

A long, long time ago
  The angels sang for joy,
For sleeping in a manger bed
  Was a little baby boy.

GIRL: Do you know why Jesus
    Was so special?
    Because He was *God's* baby!

BOY 2: *(Carrying a hammer)*

When Jesus was a little boy,
  He played and went to school.
He learned to be a carpenter
  And use His daddy's tools.

GIRL: Do you know why Jesus
    Was so special?
    Because He was *God's* little
    boy.

BOY 3: *(Carrying a cross)*

When Jesus was a grown-up man,
  He made blind people see.
He taught us how we ought to live
  And He died for you and me.

GIRL: Do you know why Jesus
    Was so special?
    Because He's *our* Jesus!

—Marita M. Root

A Little Mighty Person

I'm a mighty little person *(pause)*
No. I'm a little *mighty* person,
  Compared to all of you,
But I can stand up here and say,
  "Merry Christmas. I love you too."

—Helen Kitchell Evans

We Wish You a Happy Birthday

*(Sung to the tune of "We Wish You a
Merry Christmas")*

We wish You a Happy Birthday.
We wish You a Happy Birthday.
We wish You a Happy Birthday,
Dear Jesus, the King.

We all know You came to save us.
We all know You came to save us.
We all know You came to save us
And soon will return.

—Wanda E. Brunstetter

The Greatest Gift

The very first Christmas gift came
    down
    From heaven up above,
Wrapped not in fancy paper
    But in our Father's love.

He put it not beneath a tree
    Trimmed all in red and gold.
He just laid Him in a manger,
    In a stable, drab and cold.

For God so loved this world of ours,
    His only Son He gave,
That through this precious little gift
    Those who believe are saved.

O measure not a present's worth
    By the money that was spent,
But by the thought and spirit
    In which the gift was sent.

So, have a happy holiday
    And lift your praise above,
For the greatest gift you'll ever get,
    Was sent from God, in love.

—*Sondra Robertson*

Behold

"Behold," the angel told Mary,
    On that day long ago,
"You will have a Son, named Jesus,
    Who all the world will know."

"Behold," the angel told the shep-
    herds,
    As they watched with awe and
    fright,
"A Babe is born in Bethlehem,
    In a lowly manger this very night."

Behold, there came wise men,
    Who followed the star on high,
Leading them to the Christ child,
    Where the star stopped in the sky.

—*Wanda E. Brunstetter*

On the Bethlehem Road

They came in twos
    Threes, and more
On their long journey
    To fill Caesar's store.

It was tax time,
    And throughout the land
People went into the city
    To obey the command.

The shepherds on the hillside
    (At the close of day)
Watched the weary travelers
    As they passed that way.

Down the dusty road
    Joseph and Mary traveled too.
She rode upon the donkey—
    (Each went to pay his dues).

They entered Bethlehem
    As stars twinkled bright.
Alas, the rooms were all filled.
    The stable was their shelter that
    night.

Suddenly in the calmness
    Of the country and the town—
Heavenly voices proclaimed the holy
    birth
    As rays of the brightest star shone
    down!

—*Lorene Beeler*

11

It's Grandmother Now

In a little, white house
At the edge of the wood
  Sitting there by a dim little light
Is a lady quite old
And she lives all alone.
  By her window she sits every
    night.
Although the snow falls,
And the winds chill her house,
  In her heart there is always a glow
As she thinks of the boys
She was privileged to rear
  And then watch into manhood
    grow.
When Christmastime comes
In this little, white house
  Every day of the past lives some-
    how.
Once again she can hear
Little tots calling her,
  But she answers to "Grandmother"
    now.

—Helen Kitchell Evans

A New Year

It is not the lights of the Christmas
    tree
  That bring a few moments of joy,
It is the birth of the baby Jesus,
  The little Christmas boy.

It is Christ coming into the world
  Giving light for all who will see;
Christ bringing hope to all human-
    kind,
  Then giving His life for you and
    for me.

May we live to honor His coming,
  Rid the world of destruction and
    fear;
May we catch a glimpse of God's
    glory
  As we enter another new year.

—Helen Kitchell Evans

Bethlehem

Oh, little town of Bethlehem,
  We see thee as of old,
Dusty streets, narrow lanes,
  Stalls where you bought and sold.
Least among the cities,
  Naught of earthly fame,
Save as David's birthplace,
  Just a hamlet on the plain.
Oh, little town of Bethlehem,
  Renowned over all the earth,
Shrine of countless millions,
  The place of our dear Savior's
    birth.

—Elizabeth Craig Haynes

The Christmas Story

My father sat within his chair,
  His Bible placed upon his knee,
And living words flowed through the
    room
  To bring the love of God to me.

The Christmas story gently told
  Of Mary, young and pure of heart,
Of angels' visits in the night,
  Of Joseph's kind and loving part.

My father's voice grew wondrous
    bright
  As shepherds heard the angels
    sing.
An awesome stillness filled the room
  As wise men knelt and kissed their
    king.

My father's troubled tones revealed
  The tragedy of Herod's plan,
The journey to a foreign place,
  The dream that led them home
    again.

So carefully my father read
  Of God's protective, loving plan,
Of Joseph, Mary, and the Boy;
  Of God, who had become a man.

—Barbara A. Hanson

12

The Innkeeper

"No room in the inn," is what the man said,
  Not a single room, or even a bed,
No place for Mary to rest her head,
  "No room anywhere," the innkeeper said.

The innkeeper didn't know when he sent them away,
  That the baby Jesus would be born on that very day,
He told Joseph of a barn where they could go and stay,
  Where Mary could have her baby in the straw and hay.

The shepherds came to visit Jesus' lowly bed,
  And knelt beside the manger where He lay His head,
The King could have been born in a more appropriate bed,
  If the innkeeper hadn't said, "Use the barn instead."

—Wanda E. Brunstetter

Christ in Christmas

No one will ever find a way
To take Christ out of Christmas Day;
No matter how the glitter shines
Within the heart of all, there pines
A great desire for love
That can only be given by God above.

There's a special joy that fills the air
At Christmas when we kneel in prayer;
There's an extra gleam in children's eyes,
There's a special star in the ageless skies;
There's a wonder that surrounds Christmas Day;
No one will ever take that away.

—Helen Kitchell Evans

Christmas Is the Season

Christmas is the season of love and joy,
When excitement fills the heart of every girl and boy.
Christmas is the season of goodwill and cheer,
A time to send fond wishes to loved ones far and near.

We celebrate Christmas, a very glad time,
With evergreen trees, boughs of holly, and holiday rhymes.
We celebrate Christmas, a most wonderful season,
But let us remember, Jesus is truly the reason!

—Wanda E. Brunstetter

Christmas Spirit 19__ (Current Year)

A Sketch for Juniors

by Helen F. Smith

Cast:
>JEFF, a skeptical boy
>DEBBY ⎫
>KATHY ⎬—Three girls on a goodwill tour
>POLLY ⎭

Time: The present year in the evening

Scene: Any outdoor winter properties may be used, or simply a background curtain with several stars hanging down

(The three girls come in dressed in winter clothes with arms full of packages. They are rather breathless and set their packages on the ground to rest their arms. They stand looking happily up at the stars when JEFF, also in winter clothes, enters looking dejected.)

JEFF: What in the world are you girls standing there stargazing for? Girls are so silly.

KATHY: We are thinking about some wise men that followed a star once.

POLLY: They brought gifts to the Christ child. These are gifts in our packages.

DEBBY: It helps our Christmas spirit.

JEFF: Christmas spirit! That was almost 2,000 years ago. What do you think you are going to do . . . follow some star with all those packages?

(Girls laugh)

DEBBY: Well, not exactly, but Jesus said if we help some of His brothers, we are helping Him too.

KATHY: So we are taking these things to people who need them. I think Granny Moore needs this pretty wreath for her door. *(Holds up wreath)*

POLLY: And I have mittens and this plant to deliver. *(Indicates items)*

DEBBY *(lifting potato bag):* These potatoes are heavy, but we raised them. I know Mr. Brown's family can use them.

14

JEFF *(looking at ground):* What are the rest of these packages for?

KATHY: Over there is a pie . . . a cherry pie . . . for old Mr. Pike.

POLLY: Those are carrots. Mrs. Grey is sick and has to eat lots of vegetables.

DEBBY: I have milk for the Jones children.

JEFF: Well, I think those wise men were rich, and you girls have all the gifts. I don't have *anything* . . . and I don't have any Christmas spirit either!

DEBBY: Oh, Jeff, you do not need anything. Just pretend you are a camel and carry our things! Here are the potatoes. *(She picks up the bag and hands it to him.)*

JEFF *(looks surprised, then reaches out, takes the potatoes, and flings them over his shoulder):* Yes, I suppose I can be a camel. These potatoes will make a good hump!

KATHY: Oh, yes. Take this wreath. *(Puts it quickly around his neck)*

JEFF: I'd rather have the pie!

KATHY: Camels don't eat pie, silly.

POLLY: Here, take these carrots too. But don't eat them! *(Puts bag into his other hand)*

(Girls pick up rest of packages and go offstage. JEFF *follows bent over with his gifts, good-humoredly.)*

How Jesus Came

A Two-Scene Christmas Play in Verse for All Ages

by Judith McFerren

Cast:

MARY
JOSEPH
SHEPHERD 1
SHEPHERD 2
WISE MAN 1
WISE MAN 2

WISE MAN 3
KING HEROD
PRIEST
SCRIBE
JESUS, two-year-old, nonspeaking part
ANGEL

Scene 1

(All actors enter from the same side. On the opposite side of the performance areas should be a manger with child and a low stool behind it. MARY and JOSEPH enter.)

MARY:

> I remember an angel came
> To tell me I'd have a child.
> He even told me the baby's name,
> Jesus, Son of the Highest.

JOSEPH:

> The angel came to see me too,
> And told me not to fear.

MARY:

> The time came when the Child was due.

JOSEPH:

> And a census was taken that year.

MARY:

> So I went with Joseph, on a donkey's back.
> But in Bethlehem we lacked.

JOSEPH:

> We were given a place where animals lay,
> So Jesus was born where God did say.

16

(MARY and JOSEPH move to the side, behind the manger. SHEPHERD 1 and SHEPHERD 2 and any additional enter. Lines may be divided differently if desired. One should carry a stuffed or cardboard lamb.)

SHEPHERD 1:
> We were out in the fields that night
> When the sky was filled with a glorious light.

SHEPHERD 2:
> And an angel brought us a brand-new joy,
> Our Savior had come as a baby boy.

SHEPHERD 1:
> So we hurried off to Bethlehem,
> And in a stable we found Him.

SHEPHERD 2:
> Then we went and told everyone
> That God had sent for us His Son.

(SHEPHERDS move off toward MARY and JOSEPH and stand behind them. If there are several shepherds, one or two could kneel to one side of the manger. MARY picks up the baby.)

MARY:
> I thought about everything in my life,
> About glorious angels, and donkeys, and hay,
> How God kept me safe as Joseph's wife,
> At what my Son would do someday.

SHEPHERD 1:
> Tonight God's love does all surround.
> Let us tell all the people around.

(All exit. JOSEPH picks up stool. The last two SHEPHERDS carry out manger.)

Scene 2

(Where the manger had been, there is now a low table with one chair behind it. On the side where the actors enter is a throne. KING HEROD is sitting on it.)

KING HEROD:
> They told me they came to see a king.
> To worship Him whose star they'd seen.
> I told them that I'm the king.
> I want to know just what this means.

(PRIEST and SCRIBE and any additional enter carrying scrolls, which they unroll and examine as they speak.)

PRIEST:
> We've found the records of a king,
> Our scrolls have told us everything.

SCRIBE:

> The ruler of Israel will be born
> In Judaea; so it is written.
> The prophet wrote in time long gone
> That Bethlehem would honor be given.

PRIEST:

> From the seed of David shall come
> The Christ, God's Holy One.

(The priests and scribes exit. WISE MEN *enter.)*

KING HEROD:

> Come and tell me, men from afar,
> When first you saw this star.

WISE MAN 1:

> For two years almost
> We've followed the star.

KING HEROD:

> Continue to search, then let me know
> That I may worship Him also.

©1990 VOLK

WISE MAN 2 *(points over the heads of the audience):*
>There is the star,
>The way we should go.

*(*WISE MEN *exit into the audience, using an aisle as their path. As they go,* KING HEROD *exits.* MARY *and the two-year-old* JESUS *enter and walk across the stage to the table.* MARY *sits. She holds* JESUS *on her lap. The* WISE MEN *time their walk to head back to the stage and walk onstage just after* MARY *is seated. They place their gifts on the table.)*

WISE MAN 3:
>For many months we've traveled far,
>Following the Jewish king's star.
>We met a king who's not the one,
>But God led us to this humble home.

*(*WISE MEN *kneel.)*

WISE MAN 1:
>We bring Him gifts as we were told.
>Because He's a king, I bring Him gold.
>Frankincense and myrrh are also here.
>Later their meaning will be clear.

(They exit. JOSEPH *enters and walks over to the table.)*

JOSEPH:
>Mary, God has warned me too.
>Egypt is safer for Jesus and you.
>When Herod is dead, then God will tell
>Us to come home to Israel.

(All leave down the aisle, through the audience and out of the room. While they are leaving PRIEST *and* SCRIBE *remove the throne, table, and chair.* ANGEL *enters.)*

ANGEL:
>This is what happened when Jesus was born,
>A story you've all heard many times,
>But its meaning is never too worn
>And never heard too many times.
>So now if you'll join our Christmas love,
>We'll all sing praises to God above.
>If the music will start up now,
>Our actors will come up for a bow.

(Play "Away in a Manger" as the actors return and bow. The actors can then lead the audience in the song.)

Plays and Programs for All Ages

Isaiah and Shear-Jashub

by David S. Lampel

Cast:
  ISAIAH
  SHEAR-JASHUB

(ISAIAH *and his son,* SHEAR-JASHUB, *enter from stage right. Travel spotlight follows them.)*

SHEAR-JASHUB *(tugging on* ISAIAH's *sleeve):* Father?

ISAIAH *(with tender impatience):* What is it, Son?

SHEAR-JASHUB: How can a baby be all of those things? How can a baby be a "mighty God"?

ISAIAH *(feigning displeasure):* You were listening again at the Temple. What must I do to keep you in school?

SHEAR-JASHUB: But Father, the Temple *is* my school. I want to be like you when I become a man.

ISAIAH: Sit down, Son. *(They sit on step.)* Sometimes you say things that cause my heart to sing. *(Pause)* Ask what you will; I will answer.

SHEAR-JASHUB: When you were preaching in the Temple, you told the men that a baby would be born—and you described Him with names and words sounding more like a king than a baby.

ISAIAH: Every king that ever was and ever will be was once a baby. Their power is not diminished by that.

SHEAR-JASHUB: But Father, you made it sound as if *this* baby would be God himself. How can that be?

ISAIAH *(placing his arm around his son's shoulders):* If you are to grow in the wisdom of the Lord, you must first open your heart to Him. No one—not even I—can understand everything the Lord God tells us. But if we are to hear His voice at all, we must listen with our hearts. *(He stands and continues)* God spoke to me. He instructed me to tell the people: "A child will be born, a son given to us; the government will be on his shoulders; we will

20

call him Wonderful Counselor, Mighty God, Everlasting Father . . . Prince of Peace."

SHEAR-JASHUB *(quietly, seriously):* What do you think it means, Father?

ISAIAH: It means we are people walking in darkness, and God is going to send Someone who will light the way. It means we can't handle it on our own. God will send us a Counselor—an understanding Father who will bring us peace. *(Pause)* And He will be a King.

SHEAR-JASHUB: King of our *land?*

ISAIAH: King of our hearts.

(May follow with a song.)

God's Gift—Our Gift

So many years ago, God sent His gift of love,
A tiny baby boy came to earth from heaven above.
This gift of love was a gift of life,
Sent to do away with all sin and strife.
God's Son came to free all men,
To cleanse the sins that ever have been.
God's gift was a lamb without a single spot,
Betrayal by His own was the price that was bought.
Delivered up to die on Calvary's tree,
God's own sacrifice for you and for me.
In agony and pain He suffered and bled,
Taking each of our punishment, He died in our stead.
But His death was not the end we are told,
The Bible says that on the third day He arose.
The Son of God came back to life again,
So that those who believe would be forgiven of their sins.
God's gift was much greater than any deserves,
That is why Christmas is a holiday Christians observe.
We too have a gift that we can give our King,
Our hearts and our lives we can surely bring.
Asking for forgiveness for all of our wrongs,
Our hearts becoming clean as each of us longs.
Worshiping and serving Christ in every word and deed,
Telling others of His love as we plant the seed.
Praising Him and trusting for each day that we live,
This is the greatest gift that we could ever give.
God's gift—our gift are really two in one,
Jesus in Him, and Jesus in me—He reigns in our hearts—
God's very own Son!

—*Wanda E. Brunstetter*

The Story of the Innkeeper's Son

by Nanette Purcell

Cast:

> BENJAMIN, the innkeeper's son
> DEBORAH
> SAMUEL
> NARRATOR

(May be used along with a traditional Nativity scene that will be included in notes. If Nativity scene is used, cast will need to include Joseph, Mary, Shepherd, etc. DEBORAH and SAMUEL enter stage left and carry on conversation as BENJAMIN enters stage right.)

BENJAMIN: Deborah! Samuel! Boy, am I glad to see you guys. I've got some really exciting news to tell you! Lots of unusual things have been going on here. Come on into the inn, and I'll tell you all about it!

(ALL move to stage right, to the inn.)

SAMUEL: Does this have something to do with why all of these strangers are in town?

DEBORAH: Yeah, fill us in. I want to know what they're all doing here in our town. I mean, just yesterday, Daddy told us we couldn't play by the street because there are too many people around here.

SAMUEL: I know how you feel. It is almost impossible to even run errands for Mama, since all of these people keep coming in. Benjamin, do you know what's going on?

BENJAMIN: Well, Mama said it was something about *(stammering)* Cae- ... Cae- ... Caesar Aug- ... Aug- ... Augustus wanting to count all the people in the country. I don't know why, but she said that all of the people have to go to the town of their families from long ago to be counted. That's why all of these people are here in Bethlehem.

(NARRATOR reads Luke 2:1-5 while Mary and Joseph come down right side aisle slowly toward the "inn.")

DEBORAH: So, Benjamin, tell us your good news! What's so exciting? You're positively beaming!

BENJAMIN: There are some really special visitors here in Bethlehem! I have seen them, and watched them, and I know they are extraordinary!

SAMUEL: What's so great about them? Are they staying here? Let's go see them!

BENJAMIN: Well, here goes. Be patient, and I'll try to tell you the whole story. The visitors are a man named Joseph from Nazareth and his wife, Mary. They came to the door awfully late several nights ago, looking for a place to sleep. Mary was expecting a baby, and she looked so tired. Mama tried to find some extra place for them, but the inn was so full that we already had people sleeping on the floor. She didn't want to turn them out into the cold, but she had no choice! Then I thought about the stable. I said, "Mama, at least the stable is clean and dry, and the straw would make a nice bed. Could they stay out there?" Mama said that would be fine. I gathered up some extra blankets and led the way out to the stable, putting their donkey in another stall. Then I left because they needed to sleep.

(NARRATOR *reads Luke 2:6-7 as Mary and Joseph arrive at the inn and are pointed the way to the stable at stage left.* SHEPHERDS *move down left aisle until nearly to stage.*)

BENJAMIN: Bright and early the next morning, I took the visitors a bucket of cold, clear water for them to drink, and guess what! Mary had had her baby! He was a tiny little boy, and He was all wrapped up in one of our blankets!

SAMUEL: Well, this is nice and all, but is that all you were excited about? Just a baby?

DEBORAH: Yeah, Benjamin, a baby is sweet and cuddly, and I am sure He looked quite precious, but I have never seen you act that way about a baby! You act like you saw a king or something.

(NARRATOR *reads Luke 2:8-9, then* ANGEL *says verses 10-12.* NARRATOR *reads Luke 2:13-14.*)

BENJAMIN: Well, there is more, but now you probably don't want to wait long enough to hear it.

DEBORAH: Oh, go ahead. We'll listen, we promise. Please finish your story.

SAMUEL: Yeah, we're sorry.

BENJAMIN: OK. When I got out to the stable with the water, there were a group of shepherds there looking at the baby. I asked one of the younger shepherd boys why they were in town so early in the morning, still dark, in fact. He said they had been visited by a company of angels! He explained how the angels proclaimed this baby was the Savior, the Messiah that was promised years ago!

DEBORAH: Benjamin, are you serious? We have all been told about the Messiah! Do you think the shepherd boy was telling the truth? Did the angel really say that?

SAMUEL: Oh, this is great! What else?

BENJAMIN: Well, the angel told the shepherds where to find the Baby, whose name is Jesus, and how to recognize which was the right one.

(NARRATOR *reads Luke 2:15a, then* SHEPHERD *says 15b.* NARRATOR *reads Luke 2:16-18, then verse 19 very slowly.* NARRATOR *reads Luke 2:20 as* SHEPHERDS *leave.)*

BENJAMIN: So the shepherds decided to come see the Baby that would be the promised Messiah!

DEBORAH: Oh, Benjamin, just think. The Messiah—born right here in Bethlehem, our quiet little Bethlehem! Let's go out and see Him!

(NARRATOR *reads Matthew 2:1-11a, as* WISE MEN *come up right aisle and stop a little short of the stage until verse 7, the proceed slowly to stable and kneel.)*

BENJAMIN: But that's not all! A few days later, I saw a caravan come into Bethlehem, and there were some men who came to the inn looking for the Baby. They appeared very wealthy, and said they had traveled a long way to see Him. We showed them where Mary and Joseph and baby Jesus were, and then, guess what? These important, wealthy men knelt down before the Baby in what seemed like reverence! They even brought Him presents. One was *gold!*

SAMUEL: You mean real *gold?* to a *baby?*

BENJAMIN: Yes, gold. I was amazed! I told you that baby is special!

(NARRATOR *reads Matthew 2:12 as* WISE MEN *exit down left aisle.)*

BENJAMIN: Then the wise men went home, talking about a different way to go, for some reason. See, that was not just another baby! If the angels were right, this baby will be the One who will take away all of the sins of the whole world. I wonder, though, just how many people will believe Him?

(Exit.)

A Shepherd's Christmas

by Kevin Stoltz

Cast:
> PRODUCER
> DIRECTOR
> NARRATOR
> ELI
> HIRAM
> PHILLIP
> CHOIR
> SEVEN SHEPHERDS

Setting:
Regular stage. As an opening, children come onstage to decorate the area. Music should be inserted at various points, for emphasis, as marked.

(Opening song. PRODUCER, NARRATOR, *and* DIRECTOR *enter.)*

PRODUCER: And I tell you I don't like it. I don't like it one bit. Three weeks before opening night, and we still don't have a theme for this year's Christmas production.

DIRECTOR: I know I suggested this once before, but why not simply retell the Christmas story?

PRODUCER: No. Let the little kids sing their "Away in a Manger" and "O Little Town of Bethlehem"; it's the same old story told the same old way.

DIRECTOR: But that's exactly my point—it is the same old story.

NARRATOR: Same old story! You two talk as if Christmas and Christ's birth were some stuffy, two-hour sermon. The Christmas story is . . . magical!

DIRECTOR: Wait, let me finish. It is the same old story, but we don't have to tell it the same way.

PRODUCER: What do you mean?

DIRECTOR: Why don't we tell the Christmas story from someone else's viewpoint?

NARRATOR: I get it! We can tell the story as seen by another person.

PRODUCER: Such as the wise men, or Joseph and Mary, the innkeeper, the angels, . . . the shepherds!

NARRATOR and DIRECTOR: The shepherds?

PRODUCER: Yes! Let's do a Christmas play as the shepherds must have seen it.

NARRATOR: Sounds great to me.

DIRECTOR: Me too! *(Turns to choir)* All right, everyone; time to get ready for rehearsal—let's tell the story!

(Song)

DIRECTOR *(over musical interlude):* Great. Now that we're going to tell a shepherd's Christmas, where do we start?

PRODUCER: Why not start at the beginning?

NARRATOR: That's easy enough. And in the same country there were shepherds keeping watch over their flocks by night.

DIRECTOR: Shepherds! Take your places.

(ELI, HIRAM, *and* PHILLIP *come forward in bathrobes and towels over their heads.)*

PRODUCER: No! No! No! NO bathrobes and no angels with cardboard wings. Let's do something out of the ordinary. Remember, you did say it was the same story, but told in a different way.

DIRECTOR: OK. OK. Put the bathrobes in the closet, and put the wings back in the box. Quiet on the set! Shepherds take your places, and remember, we want something different.

(SHEPHERDS *face audience on different level of platforms. They act bored and tired.)*

ELI: Sure, no problem.

HIRAM: That'll be easy to do.

PHILLIP: Piece of cake.

DIRECTOR: Shepherds on the hillside, take one.

NARRATOR: And in the same country there were shepherds keeping watch over their flocks by night.

ELI: Sheep, sheep, sheep. Nothing around here for miles but stupid sheep. Twenty-four hours a day, seven days a week, in all types of weather— nothing to keep you company but a flock of stupid sheep.

HIRAM: Yep, and Eli, you've been around sheep so long, you even smell like these stupid sheep!

ELI: Yeah? Well, I might smell like sheep, but you two are dumber than the stupidest sheep.

PHILLIP: Is that so? If we're so dumb, explain how you got cheated by the Romans with your tax money last month!

HIRAM: Have you learned how to add yet, Eli? Two plus two is three, right? *(Laughs.)*

ELI: I can add just as well as you can.

HIRAM: Cannot.

ELI: Wanna bet?

HIRAM: Oh yeah?!

PHILLIP: Oh, would you two stop it for crying out loud! I've got enough to do, watching the sheep on this cold night, without having to listen to you guys quarrel.

ELI: And I'd like to get some sleep while I'm off duty.

HIRAM: Off duty? And here I thought you only slept while you were *watching* the sheep!

ELI: How would you like to *watch* my fist in your face?

HIRAM: I'd like to see you try it!

(They run at each other and start to fight—kids in choir can gasp, cheer, make noises, etc.)

PRODUCER *(running up and shouting):* Stop it! Stop it! Cut! What on earth are you guys doing?

DIRECTOR: You did say, "Do something out of the ordinary."

PRODUCER: Yes, but you can't have the shepherds fighting onstage.

PHILLIP: Why? We won't break anything.

PRODUCER: That's not the point.

DIRECTOR: The point *is,* that too often we forget that the shepherds were people just like us.

ELI: And we fight and quarrel. I mean, I know we're not supposed to, but we do argue and sometimes tease our brothers and sisters.

HIRAM: And sometimes we lie, when we know we shouldn't; I know that is wrong, but don't you think the shepherds might have had the same kind of problems?

NARRATOR: Maybe that's why they were so glad to hear the angel's news of "peace on earth." It brought them hope.

PRODUCER: Well . . . I guess you do have a point there, but I draw the line at having the angels arguing back and forth.

DIRECTOR: Agreed. No angels will be fighting—at least not while they're on-stage. OK everyone, let's pick up to the Frightened Shepherds scene.

NARRATOR: And suddenly, there was with the angel, a multitude of the heavenly host, praising God and saying . . .

CHOIR *(loud and excited, maybe sing):* Glory to God in the highest!

(Naturally the SHEPHERDS *are very frightened, and they act it.* CHOIR *sings song that announces the birth of Jesus.)*

ELI: Um . . . Um . . . Um . . . I think, maybe we should do what they said!

HIRAM: Yeeees, or they might come back!

PHILLIP: What about the sheep?

ELI: I'm going to do what they said. See you at the inn! *(Leaves)*

HIRAM *(slight pause):* I think I'll go too! *(Leaves)*

PHILLIP *(stares up at the sky while talking—does not see the others leave):* Do you want me to stay here and watch the sheep? *(Looks around)* Alone? Eli? Hiram? *(Runs offstage shouting)* Wait for me! Wait for me!

NARRATOR: And the shepherds did as it was told to them. And they found their way to the innkeeper's stable and found Mary and Joseph, and the Baby was lying in a manger, just as it was told to them.

(Song)

ELI: I saw a baby.

PHILLIP: I've seen the Baby.

HIRAM: We have seen the most beautiful Baby.

ELI: As the angels said it was, can He really be God?

PHILLIP: Is it possible for God to become a child?

HIRAM: Yes. A miracle. And we have seen Him. Wait until our families hear about this!

PHILLIP: Yes, but will they believe us?

HIRAM: Maybe. Maybe not. But I'm certainly going to tell everyone what I've seen!

ELI *(as they turn to leave):* I still can't believe it—a little baby! A little baby! I've seen a little baby, and He is the King!

(Song)

NARRATOR: And the shepherds returned glorifying and praising God for all that they had heard and seen, just as it had been told to them. They told their families, their friends, and even other shepherds all the strange and miraculous events.

(ELI, PHILLIP, *and* HIRAM *in mime, tell all of the other* SHEPHERDS *all that has taken place.* SHEPHERDS *respond out loud.)*

SHEPHERD 1 *(with* ELI): Can it be?

SHEPHERD 2 *(with* HIRAM): Impossible!

SHEPHERD 3 *(with* PHILLIP): Are you sure?!

SHEPHERD 4: What did you say?

SHEPHERD 5: Then it is true!

(ELI, HIRAM, *and* PHILLIP *exit stage.)*

SHEPHERD 1: Finally! Finally, there can be peace on earth, for God and sinners are reconciled.

SHEPHERD 2: Let the whole world proclaim with the angels—Christ is born in Bethlehem!

SHEPHERD 3: We bow before the heaven-born Prince of Peace. Hail the Son of righteousness!

SHEPHERD 4: This child brings life, light, and healing. He heals broken shepherds.

SHEPHERD 6: He heals broken people!

SHEPHERD 1: Why, He has been born that we may live and *not die!*

SHEPHERD 2: He is—Immanuel!

SHEPHERD 7: God is with us!

SHEPHERD 3 *(softly):* Come, all ye faithful. Come, the whole world, and adore Him.

(Music starts for a medley of Christmas carols.)

SHEPHERD 4: Listen. Is that the angels I hear?

(Music)

DIRECTOR: Ready on the set for "Changed Shepherds, scene 3."

NARRATOR: For God so loved the world that He gave His only Son, that whoever believes in Him, should not die, but have—

ALL: —everlasting life.

PHILLIP: We are changed shepherds.

HIRAM: We'll never be the same, now that we have encountered this child.

ELI: I'll never get bored with watching sheep, that's for sure!

PHILLIP: Well, I don't know about that. I doubt if we'll see angels every night. But now since we've met the Jesus child, being a shepherd sure seems to take on more meaning.

HIRAM: I think I'll remember this night for a very long time.

ELI: I wonder if other people will?

PHILLIP: It's hard to tell. People usually remember things best when they have experienced them.

ELI: I wonder how other people could experience tonight?

PHILLIP: I don't know. But somehow I think the infant King Jesus could make it possible.

(Song)

PRODUCER: Well, I must say I certainly like the production so far.

DIRECTOR: Now all we need is a finale.

PRODUCER: Yes. Let's see . . . in the last scene, the shepherds have already gone back to their families and friends because Christmas has changed their hearts, so we could . . . No, that won't work.

DIRECTOR: Why couldn't we . . . No, that won't work either.

NARRATOR: How about this: Since we're telling Christmas as the shepherds experienced it, why not end with a number that would encourage the audience to see themselves as shepherds?

DIRECTOR: Great idea!

PRODUCER: Do you think it'll work?

NARRATOR: Sure! We can go back to the part when the angels first appeared to the shepherds.

DIRECTOR: And instead of having shepherds onstage, we'll address the people in the audience as if they were the shepherds.

NARRATOR: Exactly!

PRODUCER: I get it now! By having the audience see themselves as shepherds, maybe they'll respond to Christmas as the shepherds did.

DIRECTOR and NARRATOR: Right!

DIRECTOR: OK, everyone, get ready for the finale.

NARRATOR *(to audience):* We are all shepherds keeping watch in the night.

SHEPHERD 1 *(to audience):* You are shepherds, keeping watch in your night.

NARRATOR *(loudly):* Waiting!

SHEPHERD 1 *(pause, softer):* Waiting.

NARRATOR *(pause, softer):* Waiting.

(Long pause. When the CHOIR *speaks, they should startle the people just as the shepherds were jolted. Remember, they have to sound like a million angels.)*

CHOIR: Do not be afraid, for we bring you great joy, which shall be to all people!

(Closing choir number.)

©1990 VOLK

One Night So Long Ago

C. J. R.

Caryl Johnson Rand

Flowing

1. One night so long a - go, A - mid the win - ter's snow,
2. Shep - herds who saw the light, re - joiced that ho - ly night,
3. For un - to you that day, rest - ing up - on the hay,
4. They came with haste and found Mar - y and Jo - seph 'round
5,6. Glo - ry to God on high, Glo - ry to God on high,

Je - sus, the Ho - ly Babe came.
As they were tend - ing the sheep.
The bless - ed Christ was born.
Je - sus a - sleep in the hay.
Glo - ry to God in the high - est!

All wrapped in swad - dling clothes, ly - ing in sweet re - pose,
"Fear not," the an - gels sing, "Tid - ings of joy we bring,"
Seek Him, the Ho - ly Child, of Mar - y, meek and mild,
They glo - ri - fied the Lord, gave thanks God's ho - ly Word
Sing "Al - le - lu - ia!" Sing "Al - le - lu - ia!"

6th time to Coda

1,3,4 | 2,5

And Je - sus was___ His name.
As Mar - y let___ Him sleep.
Find Him be - fore___ the morn.
Fore - tells a - bout___ this day.
Sing "Al - le - lu - ia!"

Mean - while there was a light,   Mak - ing the heav - ens
Out of the East they came,   Wise - men of splen - did

bright.   The an - gels sang in___ cho - rus,___   "Glo - ry to
fame,   Guid - ed a - long by the star.___   Bear - ing three

1st time: D.C. to vs. 3
2nd time: D.C. al Coda

CODA

God in the high - est!"___   ia!"   Sing "Al - le - lu -
gifts from a - far.___

ia!"   Sing "Al - le - lu - ia!"___

33

Joy to the World

(Children's song)

D. M.

DAVID MCDONALD

Driving ♩ = ca. 84

mf

1. Joy to the world___ the Lord has come. Joy to the world___ let
2. Glo - ry to God___ in heav'n on high. Glo - ry to God___ the

chil - dren sing. Joy to the world___ the Lord has come.
an - gels sang. Glo - ry to God___ in heav'n on high.

f

Let heav'n and earth___ re - ceive her King.
All of the bells___ in heav - en rang.

Opt. div.   cresc.

mp

Joy   to   the   world____   let   earth   re -
Glo - ry   to   God____   let   earth   re -

cut time feel

mp

cresc.

f

1   D.C.   2

ceive   her King.
ceive   her King.

mf

© 1987 VOLK

Let the Earth Now Praise the Lord

H. HELD, 1643, tr. C. WINKWORTH

RICHARD H. NEIDERHISER

1. Let the earth now praise the Lord, Who hath
2. What the fa - thers most de - sired, What the
3. Wel - come, O my Sav - ior, now! Hail! my
4. King of glo - ry, en - ter in! Cleanse me
5. As Thy com - ing was in peace, Noise - less,
6. And when Thou dost come a - gain As a

tru - ly kept His word, And the sin - ners'
proph - ets' heart in - spired, What they longed for
por - tion, Lord, art Thou! Here, too, in my
from the filth of sin. Praise to Thee, the
full of gen - tle - ness, Let the same mind
glo - rious King to reign, I with joy may

Help and Friend Now at last to us doth send.
many a year, Stands ful - filled in glo - ry here.
heart, I pray, O pre - pare Thy - self a way.
work is done; I be - long to Thee a - lone.
dwell in me That was ev - er found in Thee.
see Thy face, Tru - ly ran - somed by Thy grace.